An
UNFORTUNATE
STROKE
of
LUCK

An UNFORTUNATE STROKE of LUCK

A Guidebook
FOR STROKE SUFFERERS AND
THEIR FAMILIES AND FRIENDS

Tami Regan

Packaged by Pleasant Word, PO Box 428, Enumclaw, WA 98022. The views expressed or implied in this work do not necessarily reflect those of Pleasant Word. The author(s) is ultimately responsible for the design, content and editorial accuracy of this work.

Unless otherwise noted, all Scriptures are taken from the Holy Bible, New International Version, Copyright © 1973, 1978, 1984 by the International Bible Society. Used by permission of Zondervan Publishing House. The "NIV" and "New International Version" trademarks are registered in the United States Patent and Trademark Office by International Bible Society.

Scripture references marked KJV are taken from the King James Version of the Bible.

Scripture references marked NASB are taken from the New American Standard Bible, © 1960, 1963, 1968, 1971, 1972, 1973, 1975, 1977 by The Lockman Foundation. Used by permission.

ISBN 1-4141-0320-4
Library of Congress Catalog Card Number: 2004098458

Dedication

This book is dedicated to

Mike, Dustin, Taylor, and Trevor. I could not have survived the stroke and the following healing year without each of you. Mike, your constant love and support through each and every difficult detail has enabled me to not only survive this, but to know that life can be wonderful and happy when shared with love.

Dustin, Taylor, and Trevor, my beautiful, wonderful children; you make me complete. I have pushed on in the face of those challenges that seemed impossible because I am your Mom, and you need me in your lives to be Mom!

I love each of you deeply

Table of Contents

Foreword

I have been a part of many individual's lives following such a devastating event. The time I was able to spend with Tami Aleman was such a delightfully enlightening experience in spiritual and human strength as she fought back against the side effects of this event in her life. Her book is a fulfilling documentation of her experiences that are individual in the characters but the same in all cases. She offers very good advice, based on her experience that is practical and relationship saving. The laughter and tears you will experience when reading this book will be heartfelt, and it will leave the reader with the sense that they have just spent time with a good friend.

—Kryste Haas, OTR

What struck me the most after my first physical therapy visit with Tami was her determination. The old adage "Where there is a will, there is a way" kept popping into my head. Tami's story is not unusual, but it is unique, proof that our uniqueness as individuals does not get lost after a stroke. The path to healing, however, has to be our own. There are certain events and situations that most stroke victims will share, such as the first moment of realization, "I had a stroke," seeing friends and family for the first time, rehabilitation with speech, occupational, and physical therapy, and for those lucky ones, ultimately returning to home, work, recreational, and community life once more. For Tami, her recipe for success was a heaping of humor, dollops of determination, and finally a grudging acceptance to include pounds of patience. Tami found her path and hopefully this book will inspire you or a loved one to find yours.

—Chris Denham, PTR

Things I've learned since My Stroke

Remember to thank God for every day I'm allowed here in this life.

Cherish each of my children for the wonder that they are.

Hug and tell my dearest friends and family that I love them each time I see them.

Enjoy warm, sunny days, taking special joy in the green grass, the brilliant colors of the flowers, and the chirping birds.

My family will always truly be there for me.

Friends are my chosen family, and it's important to invest in them.

Slower is better than faster.

FOR THE FAMILY AND FRIENDS OF THE STROKE VICTIM

CHAPTER 1

The Beginning

Okay, eventually, I must find a way to begin this creation. As I always explain to my students, there is no law written anywhere that says one must begin writing at the beginning. Therefore, I've already begun this little creation with my favorite stuff to talk about: My best suggestions for success (chapter 7).

I envision several audiences for my little book, and it is divided into those appropriate sections: One: for the Immediate family and friends of the stroke sufferer, Two: for the stroke victims, themselves. Of course, I'm hoping for many readers! So here goes my little something!

My journey and new life began at 5:15 A.M. on Wednesday, November 27, 2002, while I was at bootcamp exercise class when I suffered a blood clot that somehow reached the right side of my brain, (the doctors—cardiologist and neurologist specialists are at a loss as to determine how/why the clot moved to my brain and why my body formed the clot in the first place) causing a stroke, or as the doctors refer to it, a CVA, Cerebral Vascular Accident. I always get a little giggle from that medical term. Boy oh boy, what an accident . . . . I'll wait until a later chapter (chapter12) to retell all the details of how, when, and where this "accident" happened to me as I don't imagine that the retelling of my own stroke story is important to this book because what is important is this: I have had more than several close friends, doctors, and therapists tell me that I should write about this. Not only do I trust their judgement, but I am a teacher at heart, and I would love it if others could actually benefit by reading about what I have done and learned through this experience.

Now as I see it, what I have done during these fourteen weeks since my stroke is especially to remain as positive as I possibly could and to motivate myself to strive forward even in the face of the hardest work of my life. To be perfectly honest, when I first realized I'd had a stroke, lying flat on my back in that hospital bed, unable to move my left side, I felt devastated. Nevertheless, I decided then and there that I would not let this get the best of me.

Thank God I had a wonderful life to return to. I have three beautiful, healthy, and active children who need me in their lives. I also have Mike, who I love dearly, and who loves me as perfectly as any woman could ever dream of. I have wonderful reasons to get better and return to my active life; I am also blessed with a loving circle of family and friends who have supported and encouraged me now for months. I'm still a work in process as I have not yet reached my goal of 100% recovery. That is coming this summer! I'm sure of it, and I look forward every day to that time. So, today, at 14 weeks after stroke, I am independently mobile: I walk slowly and with a bit of a left-sided limp (as therapist, Kryste says, "It ain't pretty, but it sure works!") I'm working diligently on the "pretty" part, and that's a whole story in itself (chapter 8). My average weekday involves at least two hours at warm-water-pool therapy, that I do on my own, and generally (at least once a week) an hour of one-on-one therapy with either Kryste (Occupational therapist) or Chris (Physical therapist) along with running errands, lunching with friends, picking up Trevor (my nine-year-old) from school, and finishing the day at home with hopefully a little rest, or sitting and relaxing at one of Trevor's baseball games.

Yes, I drive! On February 14, 2003, my doctor "released" me to drive. I had already begun to get cabin fever and was very restlessly unhappy with my forced dependence on others who would generously drive me wherever I needed to go. I needed the independence to be able to decide to get out and meet friends or get to the grocery store if I wanted, so I begged to be able to drive. I had practiced already with Mike and had backed out of the garage regularly in order to make room to wheel out the trash on trash days, so I was ready.

I'm very excited now about additional therapy I've been able to add several times each week at my athletic club. My trainer is easing me back into the exercise routine: lunges, squats, pushups, lots of stretching, and some weightlifting. I think the key to success is lots of work, disguised as therapy!

CHAPTER 2

Emergency Rooms, Doctors, Nurses, and Visitors

Now, I don't remember everything. Nevertheless, the really good and the really bad parts do stick out. The doctors, nurses, and visitors were wonderful; Thank God for the excellence of a reputable medical facility, staffed with caring, expert medical professionals. I remember the ambulance ride because the paramedics were very careful to continually keep me informed of everything they were doing "to/for" me. When we arrived inside the emergency room, the bombardment of questions began; here's where you can/should become better prepared than I was. Get all the appropriate medical forms (these are called Advance Directives) filled out and delivered to your local hospital, your primary care physician, and to those trusted people in your life who you can rely upon to either assist you or ultimately make medical decisions regarding your health situation. These forms can be obtained from your local hospital:

1. Living Will
2. Durable Medical Power of Attorney for Medical Decisions

I remember being asked to lie very still in order that several X-rays were done—another new experience as I'd never had an MRI or CAT scan!

The biggest decision I had to make right away was presented to Mike and me by a wonderfully, caring neurologist, Dr. Judith Vaughn, who also explained that I'd experienced a stroke, probably caused by a blood clot that had reached my brain. A wonder drug, tPa, alias—blood-clot zapper, can be administered only within three hours of the stroke onset; however, it could cause internal hemorrhage. Had I done my homework, Mike would have had his appropriate form in hand, and rather than the medical staff leaving him out in the ER waiting room, he would have been escorted in to be with me immediately. Once he was by my side, I felt so much safer, knowing that he could help me make decisions.

Guess what? It's only naturally expected that your brain and thus your ability to think clearly is a bit fuzzy right after you've had a stroke!

Next, a kind and gentle nurse informed me that she needed to "get me into" official hospital attitire— that sexy little backless gown. She asked if my workout top was valuable, so that I might prefer she not use the scissors to get it off. I said, "Cut away" because by that time I was exhausted and could care less about my workout clothes that were in no way "valuable." She carefully changed me, and put my sweaty workout clothes, cut-up top and everything else into a bag that was delivered to Mike to take care of!

I don't know if all hospitals share this "Pain Scale" terminology, but at North Colorado Medical Center, they ask you regularly to judge your pain on a scale from one to ten, with one being the lowest level and ten, the highest. Unfortunately, I developed a painful headache while in the ER. My youngest son, Trevor, picked right up on this communication, asking me regularly, "Mom, what level are you now?" He was so sweet in his genuine concern for me, and it helped him feel a part of the whole situation since he was always ready to report to anyone interested about his Mommy's "state."

A Word About Visitors . . . . Because I happened to time my little incident around the Thanksgiving holiday, and because I am blessed with a wide circle of loved ones—within a matter of hours, my gang of visitors quickly became a mob, overflowing the limited space in my ICU room and in the waiting room area. Thinking of my well-being first, Peggy, my younger sis, and Mike made the categorical decision that one person must be in charge of determining who could come to visit and the duration of that visit. Peggy said, "Okay Mike that's you—You're in charge"—"Poor Mike," I thought when this mandate was later explained to me. Nevertheless, as usual, Mike met the challenge in high style with everyone accepting his decisions. I was absolutely showered with well wishes, love, and support that I can still flashback and envision in my mind today: those loving smiles, beautiful flower bouquets, colorful, fragrant Poinsettias, and soft cuddly stuffed animals that Trev absconded with, and I think gave him something soft and warm to hang on to since Mommy had to focus on herself . . .

Just a little warning to family and friends about the "evil" Foley Catheter. Within several days, I became uncomfortably aware of the necessity of bodily functions.

Up until the time that everyone began insisting that I must use a bedpan and get my business done, I was not in the least bothered by the necessary catheter; in fact I have absolutely no recollection of the

nurses installing the horrible thing. (The doctors
had determined to treat my headache with a Mor-
phine, then Demoral drip, causing me to fall asleep
often.)

Back to the evil Foley . . . I began to experience
terrible bladder pain, feeling as if I might explode.
The nurses assured all of us that, in fact, there was
no reason for my pain, that my bladder was empty-
ing perfectly into the "evil" Foley bag. I became more
than a little disagreeable at this point which provided a round of humor to all because I can and had
been to this point, the model patient, never complaining, but always sharing a smile for everyone! I
said "Get this thing out of me now and let me go to
the bathroom on my own." I'm not kidding; I really
was in pain for some reason, and I will carry with
me forever a fear of the Foley.

Lucky for all, they removed it and helped me
get upright and settled onto a rolling commode
which was then rolled—with me happily sitting on
it—into the bathroom where I could do my business in private!

Sitting up vertically the first time, after having
been horizontal for three to four days is an experience like no other. Firstly, the stroke causes a lack
of balance and an inability to sit upright without
assistance. Mike says my face turned white then
green, which I believe because that's exactly what

my stomach was doing. This is perhaps everyone's first realization that the stroke delivers a devastating blow to the body.

However, with my resolve, we conquered the first "sitting up" and moved on to yet greater challenges.

CHAPTER 3

Do's, Don'ts, and When?

Perhaps this is the most important information to those of you who sincerely want to do whatever is best for the stroke patient. I experienced both the good do's and the bad don'ts during my hospital stay. I apologize right now to any of my loved ones who might recognize their actions in my "Don't list" as my intention is not to hurt anyone's feelings; however, if I can save the stroke patient from the bad energy of the don'ts, this information should be useful! Now, let's begin with the positive Do's!

1. If the patient is a single mother, like myself, offer to help bring her/his children to visit. Nothing lifted my spirits as much as seeing my children each day. My sister-in-law, Beth,

cheerfully picked up my children every morning before school and brought them to me so that I could send them off to school each day. Beth took them to school most of those mornings also . . . Thank you, Beth for such a wonderful gift!

2. One person should—as soon as possible—get on the phone to alert family members and close friends. (Peggy, my younger sis did the phone-calling about me) Peggy went to my house and found my phone-numbers book while I was still in the emergency room. Since all my close friends know Peggy, they were thankful to receive the call from her; thankfully, she also gave each person her phone numbers and requested that they call her for updates, rather than calling my hospital room.

3. Respect the person in charge of visitors for the patient as this person probably will spend the majority of time with the patient and will know whether or not it's a "good time" to visit.

   Many times during my hospital stay, I was exhausted and desperately needed rest/sleep time, and Mike always sensed exactly when that was!

4. Offer to take home and launder the patient's clothes. My casual/loose-fitting wardrobe, necessary for the new task of one-handed dressing, was very minimal; therefore, my hospital wardrobe needed daily laundering. Mike was again incredible, filling this job. All the female staff immediately fell in love with him as they watched him leave each night with his bag of my soiled clothes, after he'd made sure I was settled and asleep for the night. He returned every morning at breakfast with my clothes that he had laundered.

5. Someone should volunteer to "help" at every meal time because the stroke patient cannot open most of the disposable containers within which much of the hospital food is served. Again, Mike and my children filled this role for me; Mike wanted to be with me as much as possible, and fortunately his job at the time allowed for him to take all this time off.

   Nevertheless, hopefully, you're beginning to see just how much assistance a stroke patient will need throughout the duration of a hospital stay, and by offering this help up front, you will save the patient from feeling helpless and depressed, and save the patient's

"Mike" from exhaustion, from trying to do all this work!

6. Offer to "maintain" the flower bouquets and plants, sent as gifts to the hospital. These lovely gifts need regular watering and care, and it was a big job in my room! Then when it's near the time to go home, offer to transfer the flowers and plants to the patient's home. Arrange them nicely throughout the home where they can be enjoyed by all, and go back to the house regularly, to do the maintenance job because this job will be impossible for the stroke patient to perform when s/he returns home during the first few weeks!

7. Become a secretary! Bring the mail from the patient's home; open the envelopes and assist with organizing the bills and correspondence that must be handled. Help write the checks and send off the paid bills.
    (The ironic humor here is that the mortgage and utilities must be paid although the home is currently empty)
    Purchase a small notebook and record the gifts given and from whom they came because "thank-you' notes" must eventually be mailed! (See appendix A)

Make an appointment with the human resources representative at the patient's workplace and represent the patient's financial needs: sick leave must be accounted for; disability insurance forms must be filled in and sent off; check about job security!

8. If you should happen to "use" the patient's home because you're visiting from out of town, be sure to cleanup and straighten up even if there were already messes before you arrived. Launder the bed linens and re-make the beds if you use them! Wash and put away the dishes you use! How lovely it would have been for me to return to my home if someone had taken the time to come in and straighten up all the various little messes left behind by others who had "used" my home while I was in the hospital!

9. Offer to follow through on any scheduled or planned events that the stroke patient will miss because of being hospitalized.

   For example, my daughter, Taylor's 16th birthday came several weeks into my hospital stay. I had secretly been planning to throw a fun surprise party for her. My wonderful girlfriend, Roberta, took over the organizing and running around that was necessary to get the party under way. She enlisted helpers to decorate; she ordered, and took delivery of the food, and stayed there the whole evening to cut and serve the cake and perform the cleanup afterwards along with her crew of volunteers. Taylor and I simply arrived at the party and enjoyed a memorable night with all her friends. I will always be indebted to Roberta for making that special night happen.

10. A one-week working visit! One of the best gifts I received several weeks after returning home from the hospital was a one-week visit from my dear, sweet friend, Sharon, who drove a whole day's journey from Iowa. She came to help me: she shuttled me to therapy where she became my front row cheerleader, delivered Trev to school each morning, after "handling" the morning activities of getting Trev out of bed and into school clothes and breakfasted; each evening, she made sure we had dinner from the groceries she had gone and bought or from the meals delivered to my home by my amazing co-workers, laundered the piles of daily laundry, and she even filed away the growing stack of receipts and papers on top of my filing drawer—all this

with a cheery smile and robust laughter that cheered my days! Besides all the work, Sharon and I shared some wonderfully motivating chats during our week together: it was so special for me to have another woman in the house who understood and performed the daily tasks that I couldn't. Sharon even telephoned and organized a weekly schedule of girlfriends, each of whom had left phone messages about their desires "to help." The week after Sharon went back home to her own family and her paying job, the wonderful girlfriends then began showing up at my door on their scheduled days to either help get dinner on the table and then cleared and cleaned up or on Saturdays to help carry the laundry baskets to the laundry room and then fold and hang clothes from the dryer. (I preferred to load the laundry in the washer myself, but the folding, hanging, and putting away was too big a job for my first weeks at home—now <4 months after stroke> this complete job is one I take pride in accomplishing myself!)

11. **OR A ONCE-A-WEEK—MAID VISIT!!
My younger sis, Peggy offered to come one late afternoon each week to be my personal

maid. She said, "Make a list, and I'll go through that list and get things done!"

One day the cat had vomited on the carpet in the TV room, so she cheerfully cleaned up that lovely little deposit. She helped me fold and put away several loads of laundry, and we fixed and ate a yummy dinner with my children. Then she helped get Trev to bed and settled for the night in order that I could go to bed early for a much needed rest.

12. Offer to have the patient's elementary-aged children to your home to play with your own children. I had several good friends who took Trev into their homes, especially on snowed-in Saturdays. He completely enjoyed getting out for some fun, and I thoroughly enjoyed the quiet solitude, knowing that he was safe and happy.

    **A note to neighbors—invite the child to your home rather than allowing the neighborhood gang to congregate at the stroke patient's home; I sure appreciated the times Trev was safe and happy at the neighbor's rather than the neighbor boys "safe and happily cared for" by me in my home.

13. Rather than sending the "goodie basket" gift to the hospital, hold off until the patient returns home! While the gifts were wonderful to receive during my stay in the hospital, I truly appreciated those I received once I had been home several weeks. What a special treat it was to receive the delivery of a basket filled with scented soaps, yummy snacks, and other pampered items to brighten those sometimes dull, dreary days at home!

14. Organize a schedule of dinners to be delivered to the patient's home after s/he has returned home. I work with a large staff of teachers who were just itching to do whatever they could to help out, so my friend, Roberta devised the wonderful idea of scheduled dinners for my little family. These were so appreciated because nobody in my house felt like planning and cooking dinner every night! The meals were delicious and such a fun surprise to see who would show up at the door each evening.

DON'T   DON'T   DON'T
     DON'T   DON'T
     DON'T

OKAY, UNFORTUNATELY THIS HAS TO BE SAID BECAUSE SOME PEOPLE IN THEIR OWN GRIEF WILL MAKE THESE MISTAKES.

1. Do not visit if/when the patient is tired and needs sleep.

2. Do not come to the hospital and demand to consult with the doctors. Trust that the patient's designated decision-maker is well in charge of the doctors!

3. Do not call constantly on the telephone in the hospital room unless the patient has requested you do so! Most people simply do not understand the extent of damage done to the stroke patient's body- strength and stamina. I was very tired most of the time (the whole month) I was in the hospital, initially because of the pain medication, later because, by my choice, I followed a strenuous rehab schedule every day while on the rehab floor. Talking to people on the phone was absolutely exhausting for me. I understand that loved ones "need" to hear the patient's voice; however this is not the time for others to be needy! In this day of cell phone technology, the best option is to call

the patient's "Mike" to get the necessary updates on the patient. Mike began answering his phone, "Tami's Hotline!" Remember, however, that most people do not have the patience and endurance of my Mike, and don't overdo the calls as to become a nuisance! Sit down and write a special card if you have the need to communicate, and send it to the patient's hospital room.

4. Do not plan, especially if the patient is like me, a one-week resting visit once the patient is home. The last thing I needed were "visits" from people who thought we might just quietly rest and lounge around my cozy little home. I am a busy, involved Mom with active children, and my daily schedule while they attend school involves therapy at two different facilities in town along with various doctor visits, grocery shopping, and the regular daily household tasks that must be accomplished! I needed a helper, someone who was ready to ask "What can I do to help you now?" not someone who thought s/he might enjoy a quiet week's rest at home with the "recovering stroke patient."
I don't mean to sound cruel; however, the point of this book is really to help folks un-

derstand that the road to recovery is a long, difficult, hard-work journey, followed through on a daily basis! Nothing has been "easy" for me since the stroke, but everyone comments on my amazing recovery rate! It is so important for loved ones to be "helpers," not hindrances!

FOR THE STROKE VICTIM

CHAPTER 4

"In Hospital"

et up; get to the toilet; then get to the
Rehab floor ASAP! Plan to take advantage of the excellent therapy available on
the rehab floor, knowing full well that you are beginning your journey to the hardest work of your
life. If you are satisfied to stay in bed, enjoying the
"forced" rest, the rehab floor is not the place for you;
however, if your goal is to begin the steps to recovery, rehab is where you want to be. You'll be assigned
Occupational (OT) and Physical therapists (PT) who
quickly become your very own personal drill sergeants. I soon learned that "OT" essentially means
therapists whose main focus is your upper body
(shoulder, arm, hand, fingers), and "PT's" are therapists who get you up and moving on those feet again!
Additionally, Speech Therapists are assigned to those

stroke patients who have also lost their ability to talk. I was blessed by not having this issue to deal with.

CHRISTY (OT) taught me to perform my personal grooming with only the use of my right hand, and she introduced me to electrical stimulation (E-Stim). Electrodes are strategically placed on the arm muscles; then, a light electrical current is delivered to those muscles, "reminding them that they can indeed move! Honestly folks, this does not hurt; in fact it's exciting, watching your arm moving once again! This procedure is clinically researched and proven to be highly effective for stroke patients. The strategy is that when the electric current "moves" the muscle, a neurological message is also sent back to "remind" the brain that these muscles can and do work, in effect, setting up a new pathway—backwards—from the muscle to the brain because the old established pathways have been blocked by the stroke, hence the loss of physical function on one side of the body. Today, four months from the stroke date, I continue E-stim therapy for my wrist and fingers!

On the Rehab floor, Christy and I spent hours together while she taught me how to shower one-handedly—forget about your past quickie "in and out" ten-minute showers!

Speaking of showers . . .

I have a funny story that will hopefully demonstrate the importance of making every effort to keep things light-hearted while in the hospital and how very important sisters can be! During my first week after stroke, and once I was moved off the Critical Care Unit and into a private hospital room, I decided it was high time to get my hair washed and my legs shaved. However, because of the instability caused by the stroke, the nurses would not let me shower without assistance, nor was I capable yet of showering one-handed. I needed help! Peggy, my younger sis came to the rescue! Peg brought shampoo and the necessary shaving razor, and with the help of a precious CNA, we, all three, were successful in getting me situated on the bench in the shower. Peg wore her swimsuit and her glasses so she could see her work area, and the CNA posted herself, closely outside the shower in order to hand Peggy the shampoo, conditioner, and shaving crème as needed. It was hilarious, and we all got very wet and shared lots of great giggles out of the whole production! I really needed to get cleaned up, and Peggy knew how important it was for my self-esteem.

Ladies, you know how trusting one must be to allow another person to shave your legs, and little sis is probably one of the few who could perform the job for me!

Later, on the rehab floor, I also learned to become adept at putting on socks, using just one hand—absolutely amazing accomplishments! Oh the new things to be learned!

**An important note: I had almost forgotten about this part, but Mike reminded me as he was reading through this first draft! During the first week of my hospital stay, I suddenly began feeling tingling sensations all over my left side—this tingling is very similar to the feeling when your foot has "fallen asleep" perhaps when you've been sitting for a long time reading a book or watching TV, and you decide to get up quickly to move about, but discover that your foot "fell asleep"—it feels like tiny little pinpricks—not painful, but definitely uncomfortable. What was happening was that the "feeling" sensation was returning to my left side! All the medical staff was thrilled, saying, "Tingling is good!"

Well, it was a pain-in the-butt for me! I couldn't get comfortable, especially at night to sleep. Thankfully, Dr. Amy prescribed the drug "Elavil" to take at night to relieve the tingles-sensation, and it worked, allowing me to sleep restfully! I discontinued taking it as soon as I was able to return to my regular sleep habits.

Another irritating situation that can happen while in the hospital is to be assigned a therapist who you don't get along with. I was assigned a speech therapist who I'm sure is a very nice person; however, she and I just did not click! Your therapists in

the hospital work very closely with you, and because the rehabilitation is so new and difficult for
the stroke patient, the therapists with whom one
works must also be people with whom the patient
enjoys spending time! If you should happen to find
yourself with a therapist that you are not happy with,
I suggest you talk to your rehab doctor and try to
make a switch. My doctor listened carefully to me
and agreed with my concerns, and she completely
took care of my therapist issue.

> Get out of that wheelchair . . . to the
> walker . . . . to the cane . . . . To, "Look every-
> one . . . No hands!"

Sara, my wonderful PT, challenged me to get up
and out of the wheelchair, to push the walker down
the hallway, then to switch to just a cane for support, and to actually walk from my room to the el-
evator doors in order to join the real world outside
the safety of the rehab floor.

Take "Out on Leave" respites

Of course, life "on the outside" doesn't stand still
simply because your life—as it was—has suddenly
ceased. Trevor was still playing basketball and participating in weekly games that I didn't want to miss.

My wonderfully, understanding, and insightful re-hab doctor, Amy Robbins, encouraged me to "Go; Get out!" She arranged for me to leave, to go "Out-On-Pass," but only under the careful protection of Mike, and once with my sister-in-law, Beth, who escorted me to Trev's school for his third-grade Christmas Party!

Nevertheless, first, we were instructed by OT Christy during an outdoor practice session as to the proper procedure to make my "transfers" from the wheelchair to the carseat and back again! We had some of our best laughs during this practice session when my head was accidentally bumped, and while contorting our bodies into the appropriate positions to accomplish these transfers in the easiest manner possible. What a hoot! Laughter is truly good medicine. My several trips out and away from the hospital worked wonders for my spirit, yet moving around out there is certainly a completely new challenge. People do look at and treat differently others in wheelchairs or with walkers or with canes. I prepared myself mentally for people's reactions to my wheelchair and my new condition. Lots of questions to answer! I decided to take it in stride and to not allow it all to depress me, rather to focus on my happiness at being alive and still participating in life, though somewhat limited.

GOAL "Independent in Room"

The ultimate goal that equates to your ticket out of the hospital is when the rehab doctor, nurses, and therapists determine that the time has come to "test" your independence level!

They post a check-off chart in your room that lists various skills that you must exhibit before being released to go home. Once you've completed the "tests," you are prepared to go home. These tests involve the following skills demonstration: brushing your teeth and performing other minor personal grooming necessities, dressing yourself, taking a shower, getting to and using the toilet, and finally, moving around the hospital room independently.

CHAPTER 5

Returning Home

W hen it came time to go home, Mike was very concerned about me, knowing that I probably would not take time to rest, but feel the need to jump right back in to all my regular "mommy" duties at home, so Mike and his angel-mom, Mary, offered her lovely home for me to go to rest for the first week out of the hospital. Fortunately, my children understood and agreed to the plan even though they were anxious to also return home with me. This was such a perfect set-up because I really needed to sleep for long stretches at a time which would have been impossible at my home, where the phone began ringing the hour my children and I returned. I'm one of those people who likes to be in control of her life—in case you haven't already figured that out. I was ready to decide when

I would get out of bed in the morning and when I would take my shower, not having to cue up in line as we did at the hospital! Though returning home was the perfect choice for me, it also increased the stress level in my new life as a recovering stroke victim. Stacks of mail had to be opened; dishes had to be put in the dishwasher, and of course the never-ending piles of laundry must be dealt with. Now, as I've already explained, I do have help from my wonderful support system.

Taylor, my sixteen-year-old daughter pitched right in, picking up Trev from school each day and helping to keep the kitchen in some sort of semblance, and she's been doing her own laundry since she was twelve. Nevertheless, those pesky, daily jobs that must be done and only moms seem to have eyes for (little boys' dirty socks that show up in the oddest places, empty water bottles that need to go in the dishwasher and then be refilled and placed in the refrigerator (I'm the quintessential, miserly recycler!), the recycle bin that must be placed outside for pickup on every other Thursday morning, the trash pickup every Friday morning, the mail that must be brought in and opened each day . . . etc) You moms know what I mean about the infinite tasks we perform on a daily basis that no one else would ever consider doing—those tasks that kids must think the magical house fairies perform while they are away at school all day! Anyway, I found myself having difficulty keeping my head above water once I returned home; it all becomes overwhelming, so be very careful when planning the return home. I suggest hiring a maid if you can swing it!

CHAPTER 6

Keep the Faith

During my stay in the hospital, and especially when I started wondering, "Why me?" my spirituality and belief in God as the larger, bigger force in my life saved me more than I can say from a severe depression that could have easily overcome my best self-motivated intentions. I'll be forever thankful that my mom always made sure that I attended Sunday school as a child. She also stood back and allowed me to choose my spiritual path when I was a teenager. We lived in a small town where everyone went to church on Sundays, and I embraced my Baptist church youth group completely. Today, I am so thankful for that solid spiritual base upon which I grew up. Of course there have been some wayward times in my adult life, especially when I lost my faith when my marriage of twenty years ended in divorce. I was angry at God for not answering my prayers for that marriage. But He had someone better for me in his greater plan as I have come to realize, especially after I've experienced Mike's loving care since my stroke.

My point here is that my faith in God has carried me through these very difficult months since the stroke. I would hope that you also have such a faith to lean back on.

CHAPTER 7

My Three Best Suggestions

Finally, I've made it! I'm here with my keyboard, writing my "book," just as I've promised myself that I'd do for the last several weeks. Even though I'm not at all pleased that I'm typing with only my right pointer and index fingers, I'm following my passion, which brings me to the topic of this chapter.

MY THREE BEST SUGGESTIONS FOR SUCCESS!

1. Pursue your passion
2. Count your blessings
3. Focus on your daily successes.

4. Get up; get outside, and take deep breaths of fresh air, and treat yourself to long and warm baths! Oops, I lied about only 3 suggestions, but this might be the best daily advice yet!
5. If you have the availability, go to warm water therapy at least five days each week; GO!!!

Explanations and examples:

1. While I absolutely love to write, I do not consider myself an expert writer. My passion is teaching students to write. I am a teacher at heart, and it is what I think I do best. Actually, this little book is as much meant to help and inspire other stroke "victims" like myself as well as provide my ticket into that elite circle of "those who are published," so here I am following my passion!

   The point of this example is to show you that even though because of certain "deficits" you will have as a result of your stroke, you can and should do something directly related to your passion. I promise it will, if anything, make you feel whole and spirited again.

More examples:

> Additionally, relating to following my passion, I took advantage of my neces-

sary down-time (rest and quiet) when I came home from the hospital, to read a few of the books in my "stack" that I'd been waiting and hoping for that magical "time" to suddenly appear when I might sit and relax with a well-written book. Reading is my favorite, quiet pasttime/hobby, but reading just gave me headaches and required way too much energy right after I had the stroke, during my hospital stay. This is the perfect segue to #2!!

2. Every day since the stroke is an uphill battle. It just never gets "easy." Therefore, I have motivated myself every single day by counting my blessings. Thank God for friends and wonderful, caring, loving, kind, and generous people. I have been amazed at the outpouring of love I have received since the stroke, and my sincere wish is that you will experience the same! My faith in God and mankind has been completely renewed because of this stroke. More blessings: I happen to have the most beautiful and talented three children in the world! I remind myself daily just how fortunate I am to have them in my life! I have saved one of the best blessings for last. I wish for each of you a "Mike."

Mike is my soul mate and the love of my life. From my first moments in the emergency room, Mike was there with me, loving and protecting me. He has been my rock . It is very difficult, after suffering a stroke, to make the many decisions required during the hospital stay. Plan to rely on a trusted "friend" to help make decisions and to provide a buffer and conduit between you and the hospital staff and well meaning others.

3. I can very simply lift my spirits by congratulating myself every day for simple accomplishments. For example, today is Saturday, and I have "succeeded" in doing five loads of laundry, straightened up my kitchen, made my bed, ate some breakfast which I completely made for myself, and have had several phone visits with a lovely new-found friend (Ruthann, this is the first sleep-over weekend you had Trev!) Now readers, please remember that I am, by my most basic nature, an over-achiever, and I simply give examples here to assist in your understanding of my points. Each day, you will find that you can now do something you could not— just a week ago! I have received the simplest pleasure from being able to open my mail

and then just having the strength to sit up long enough to read and peruse that daily mail. I suggest you find joy in each simple task you find the strength to accomplish each day!

4. I am a strong believer in the regenerating effects of nature. My stroke happened on November 27, 2002, the day before Thanksgiving; therefore, the weather in Colorado was just heading into a long, cold, cloudy winter. Today is March 14th, and we have for the last week experienced a warming trend, and Spring-time is teasing us with sunny days in the upper 60's and mid 70's!! Woohoo!! Bring on the heat!

   Even during January and February, I forced ("force" is the crucial word here) myself to at least bundle up with heavy coat and warm pants to walk outside to get the daily mail! I think fresh air can heal body and mind like nothing else . . . except maybe a good bath. Those warm baths relax the hurting, sore muscles that come right along with the stroke. If you've not learned the pleasure of a good long soak, treat yourself! I promise you'll become a bath connoisseur!

5. Finally, I can't say enough about the healing effects that my warm water therapy has provided for me. If you have a warm water therapy facility nearby, USE IT!!!!!!!
   This therapy is so instrumental in my success that I will devote a whole bunch more time in the next chapter, next!

CHAPTER 8

"Push the Gouda" and other Helpful Outpatient Therapy Tips Your new full-time job

Therapy is the "miracle cure" from a stroke! Even though the therapy in the hospital is absolutely exhausting, I think it is the best "drug" available for the stroke patient. I received the most renewed happiness and delight from each individual physical accomplishment during my therapy sessions. Mike and I still get very teary when we remember my first steps up and out of the wheelchair. I will forever smile each time I remember those moments when my therapists, Sara and Christy's faces lit up in delightful smiles at my accomplishments! In other words, folks . . . Therapy is not only the answer to regaining physical use, but it's also the answer to refreshing one's spirit after the devastation of the stroke.

** Informational Note to Stroke patient and loved ones! Your doctor and therapists will explain the therapy process and the manner in which your body will regain use (proximal then distal); however, a really easy way to understand it is that the "big stuff" comes back first: quadriceps and hamstring muscles in your upper legs (that top part of your leg, above your knee and below your hip joint) and the bicep muscle in your upper arm (that nice little tennis-ball-like bump that boys—like my 22-year-old son, Dustin, love to flex and show off!) Following the restorational "return" of these muscles comes the even harder work of getting back the smaller muscles and joints (triceps, ankles, and then those ever difficult fingers)

My ankle was weak and caused my foot to turn inwards while I was trying to walk, so PT-Sara and Dr. Amy suggested an apparatus called an "AFO" which is basically a hard, molded plastic device that cups the ankle and foot and straps around the lower leg calf muscle, "holding" them in a straightened position so that you can walk without also working at the control over the weak ankle and foot muscles. This contraption "fits" snugly inside your shoe and is not entirely uncomfortable, considering that it is a great "helper" for regaining mobility. Nevertheless, because I am terribly vain, I requested "something" else that wasn't quite so visible . "Angel" Sara quickly delivered a cushioned ankle brace! I was able to fit this one into my shoe much easier, and I felt much better walking around in public!

**Moving on and away from the rehab floor . . . Because of some ridiculous paperwork and insurance misunderstanding, my first week of scheduled outpatient therapy was cancelled and goofed up, leaving Mike and me to our own devices.

We continued my walking practice, at home and out in the real world; we did a little shopping and went to restaurants to meet family and friends for meals (all of these activities were not only good physical therapy, but also wonderful for my self-esteem!). Again, I must say how terribly important and supportive Mike was and continues to be for me. He shared his strength with me, holding me up and always making me smile and laugh, during these very difficult days of getting back into the world. However, I also needed to continue therapy for my arm, bicep and tricep strength and control. Here's where the Gouda comes in!

Several of my wonderful neighbors delivered to my home, one of those great Christmas baskets, filled with cheeses and beef sticks. Mike, always thinking, and adding humor to every situation, brought out the round Gouda cheese, placed it on a dish towel on the dining room table and said, "Now Tami, push the Gouda away and pull it back!" This at-home therapy exercise mimicked perfectly one of those I had been instructed to do in the hospital with Christy, OT. The idea is to engage the bicep by pulling a towel towards your body across the smooth, slippery tabletop, then to engage the tricep by pushing it away (much harder than it sounds!). The compact round size of the Gouda was perfect for me to place my hand over and do my best to "grip" it, while moving it back and forth across the table. Mike always found ingenious ways to make us both smile and laugh. It was hilariously entertaining for both of us and fun to "show off" a bit for loved ones who were also interested to see how this therapy works! We will never again be able to keep a straight face when the Gouda cheese is served as an appetizer or snack.

Eventually, I began my outpatient therapy at North Colorado Therapy Center (NCTC) which also is home to the warm water therapy pool and my amazingly helpful and caring therapists, Kryste Haas, OT, and Chris Denham, PT. Mike and I have learned to love these two people; they have helped me beyond belief with my road to recovery.

As long as the insurance holds out, I continue to see each of them at least once each week. Initially, we began with three times each week, which I highly suggest as a beginning outpatient therapy routine. Chris has helped me begin to regain a "normal" gait in my walk, by breaking down each intricate movement involved in the normal gait, from my head to my toes. Who—besides a PT—would have thought that so many of our body parts are intricately involved when we just simply step out and walk? It's absolutely fascinating! This process has taken quite some time for me because I had established the bad habit of hitching up my whole left hip and swinging my leg around in my hurry to walk sooner. Today, at 4° months since the stroke, I continue to work at perfecting a normal gait; I still walk slowly, with a sort of limp. I keep telling myself to be patient!

At the other end of the spectrum, initially, Kryste and I worked quite a bit at regaining strength in my tricep because my upper arm (bicep) had developed an annoying habit of pulling my lower arm in towards my body, especially when I got cold! (technically referred to as "bicep tone") I had to "teach" my tricep to kick in and push my arm back down to a "straight elbow" position, allowing the arm to hang freely at my side rather than creeping toward my tummy! Once we accomplished this amazing feat, we were able to move on to my wrist, hand, and fingers, again utilizing E-stim! The gripping/squeezing function came back to my hand sooner and easier than the extension (separating the fingers in the way one might do when waving hello) This therapy, Kryste tells me, could take months . . . . Oh the patience I'm learning! I won't have full use of my hand until I get the "extensor" motion accomplished in my fingers.

I do have small successes during therapy, like the days I succeed in pulling tissues from Kryste's tissue box with my left hand/fingers! Also, I "practice" therapy at home by pulling plastic pegs from a pegboard and then releasing them into a bowl . . . . It's very similar to the fine motor skills that preschool children become so engaged in during their hours at preschool . . . after all, I am also basically re-teaching myself to perform fine-motor skills just like preschoolers learn at pre-school.

This therapy that I've just told you about is very hard work, requiring tons of energy; in fact, after a therapy session that he has observed, Mike always comments about how tired he is just from the strain of watching me work so hard at these seemingly simple tasks.

Now the nicer, easier therapy can be done in the therapy pool. Chris, PT, started me off in the therapy pool by showing me walking and arm exercises to practice. He also encouraged me to purchase a pool pass and to come in on my own to do warm water therapy several times each week. Unfortunately at this point, my HMO insurance coverage ended for the stroke recovery therapy sessions. Amazingly, the HMO has determined that a total of thirty outpatient therapy sessions is adequate for stroke recovery . . . . . they are so WRONG, Wrong, Wrong.

Anyway, moving on to more positive thoughts, I developed my own workout routine in the therapy pool and have adhered to that routine at least three times each week. Kryste was so impressed with my results that she encouraged me to "write a book!" I would suggest this routine to anyone, wanting to loosen up tense muscles and/or to simply gain leg strength.

The NCTC therapy pool is well equipped with water toys and tools, so once I've walked into the water, I grab a "noodle," adjust it under my arms, and begin my "swim" to the deep end. The noodle keeps my upper body afloat, while I propel through the water, utilizing the frog-like breast stroke kick that I learned as a child at swimming lessons. Once I reach the wall at one side of the deep end, I begin my laps, crossing the pool, back and forth, all the while staying in the deep end . . . . not a true, full lap in the athletic sense, but a lap, nonetheless! In order to keep things interesting, I then flip over to my back to complete the lap, returning back to the other wall, crossing the noodle over the trunk of my body, holding onto it with each of my hands, (good hand therapy too!) flutter kicking all the way! I admit to thinking to myself as I'm flutter kicking away, "Tight butt, tight legs, tight tummy!" Great exercise for tightening up all the places we girls continually need to tighten!

INJURIES and maladies: Unfortunately, this has to be discussed.

I have become convinced that I was "blessed" with my injuries in order that other stroke victims who read this book won't be able to say, "But Tami really doesn't understand what I'm going through because she didn't have to deal with the unfortunate complication of injury resulting from the stroke." So here's my whiney "complication" story: During the month of March—two months after the stroke—two painful complications "happened" to me. I began waking up every morning feeling as if I had the flu, and by late afternoon each day, I again felt flu-like symptoms: nausea, aching, sore muscles, and extreme fatigue. I just wanted to go to bed. I had also developed a painful muscle injury in my left shoulder/deltoid muscle area, but only when I lifted my shoulder or arm too high.

A consult with my primary care physician resulted in the diagnosis of a stress ulcer that was causing my stomach problems, so I have adjusted my diet to that of a careful, bland ulcer diet and added yet one more pill (Prevacid) to my daily drug repertoire. Most of the time this helps, but I still have stomach problems at times that impede my progression towards the recovery I want so terribly.

Doctor Amy, rehab doc, ordered an MRI in order to better look at my shoulder problem, and on April 2nd I was informed that I have a torn rotator cuff, hence the pain in my left shoulder. For my own personal reasons, I am completely opposed to a surgical procedure to "fix" this problem, so I've begun my search for healthier alternative methods to heal the muscle. I convinced everyone that I feel sure I can continue my stroke therapy that involves both the use of the warm water therapy to loosen my muscles and joints and the concentrated OT therapy, working on my wrist, hand, and fingers. Also, I continue the gym workout with my wonderful trainer, Kim McMurran, focusing on regaining strength in my legs, combined with cardiovascular workouts.

Kim and I meet twice each week. First we stretch all the tight muscles. Then we move on to some balance and coordination exercises, then to the hard stuff: lunges and squats! I have also been using the stair-climber on my own in order to try to regain some of the cardiovascular strength I've lost due to months of missing boot-camp class. All this therapy does wonders for my inner spirit too. I feel so good about "me" once I've finished these workouts, and my stomach problems seem to disappear while I'm working out!

CHAPTER 9

Therapy Pool Etiquette

I'm amazed that I even feel the need to write this chapter; however, more than once while I've attempted to simply mind my own business and move about the pool, working through my therapy routine, I've been unable to do what I need to do because of fellow pool users who don't follow what I consider to be simple polite behavior. I've given them names and will explain my suggested etiquette rules, making my way through the assorted pool characters:

Floaters: Now there's nothing wrong with simply indulging oneself by floating around in the soothing, relaxing warm water, but the etiquette issues arise when the floater slips into la-la land, completely unaware of the

E*xercisers*, like me who are trying to swim laps. Here's the rule: If you are a *Floater*, please *float*, out of the path of the *Exerciser*.

Yackers: The *yackers* usually also double as *floaters*, but congregate in gangs, chatting and floating aimlessly about! Again, I think it's absolutely wonderful that so many folks have discovered the healing effects of warm water therapy pools; however, polite etiquette seems to call for some natural rules of politeness: On the days one comes to the pool to be a *yacker*, please *yack* out of the way of the *Exercisers!*

Exercisers: These fall into two categories: the *Movers and the Shakers*

Movers: I am a *mover* as I've explained my therapy pool routine already; you might recollect that a *mover* is a pseudo-lap-swimmer, swimming slowly back and forth, from wall to wall. Now, I've also seen *movers* behave inappropriately, attempting to swim "real" laps from shallow end to deep end during an "Adult, Open— Swim" session. North Colorado Therapy Pool offers special "Lap Swim" sessions for those who want to swim real laps, and "I say!" the *lappers* really ought to use that designated time rather than scaring off the regular, less aggressive crowd that comes to "Open— Swim"

Shakers: These are the really scary, dangerous ones! *Shakers* move fast and powerfully through or in-and-out of the water, causing waves. I've experienced the scare from shakers who attach themselves to a stair/ladder in the deep end of the pool and pull themselves up and out of the water, then bend their knees and Kaboom/splash their backends back into the water—up and down they go, exercising their legs and causing minor tidal waves with each repetition. Of course, they have no idea if a *floater* or a *mover* is behind them because, in their up-and-down frenzy, their eyes are facing the wall, not the pool and its inhabitants!

While completing one of my mini-laps, flutter-kicking along one day, I nearly ended up with a *shaker's* bottom landing on my tummy as he performed his mighty kaboom/splash back down into the water. Now, I had done my etiquette job of turning and looking to see that my return path was clear in order that I could flip to my back and safely make my lap-return to the wall. The *shaker* had not begun his shaking maneuvers, but had simply attached himself to the stair-ladder. I had mistaken him for a *floater*, thinking he would stay put, simply floating/hanging from the stairs! Fortunately, half-way through my lap, I felt his waves and realizing the danger I might be heading into, I stopped and turned to my front side to double-check my path before becoming body slammed by the *shaker! Shakers* also move through the water with flippers on their feet and hard-molded plastic devices on their hands that really hurt when you get accidentally kicked or punched because you've crossed into their "space" or as I think of it—they have invaded my space!

Actually, that's what it's all about in the therapy pool—*Personal Space*—and paying careful attention to each swimmer's space that s/he has scoped out for the day's activity, whether it be *floating, yacking, or exercising!* These are large pools, and there is room for everyone as long as each person abides by the simple and polite rules of personal space that we all learned in kindergarten!

**Readers, please do not feel intimated about using the therapy pool because of my silly "name game" terminology because this is simply my attempt at a bit of humor added to what has been a wonderful healing experience for me, and I hope it could be for you too!

CHAPTER 10

"I Think I Can; I Think I Can!

Climb the stairs, using one leg for each step at a time, and then carry in your hands a glass of water or a bag of laundry while climbing those stairs! I encourage you to set simple goals such as these that I set for myself and in which found such satisfaction once conquered.

Remember, you need to pat yourself on the back from day to day for your accomplishments, so if you don't set attainable goals, how will you be able to feel good about yourself? I'm a strong believer in goal setting and the satisfaction received from a completed job! If you have never done this in your life, try first to write your goals for each day in a little notebook, or better yet, get really organized and purchase and use a day-timer calendar. It feels great to put that little checkmark next to your jobs-for-the-day list, and to see how much you've accomplished.

Be careful though, if you've never been an avid list-maker, you might be tempted to make too long a list or write tasks on your list that are just way too ambitious—be reasonable with your daily goals, remembering the importance of feeling good about jobs well done and completed! For instance, I love to garden, but I'm not sure yet that my left hand is going to be ready for the Spring plantings next month, so I'm not setting myself up for failure by planning for my usual early May flower bed planting; I'm simply planning to do all that at some point during the summer when my hand and fingers begin to cooperate! Now are you beginning to hear the teacher/trainer in me?

I apologize if I'm sounding like I have all the answers, because I know I don't. However, I do believe in the concept of "Plan your work, and work your plan." I think, especially in the case of stroke recovery, that the stroke patient must set goals and plan for recovery!

Becoming WHOLE again

April 5, 2003—I'm not ready to write this part yet, but I know in my heart that I will by this summer. This thought about feeling whole again occurred to me yesterday when I was doing my at-home E-stim therapy. I wondered, "Will I actually feel whole again?" I do not feel that way today because I still have a lot of time and work ahead to fully recover. I am saddened at times when I miss the once easy nonchalant coordinated movements of my fit and healthy body. Coordinated movement used to be so easy for me, and I miss terribly that ease of motion. However, I am more than convinced that all this has happened to me because I am now meant to help and inspire others who will suffer from strokes. It is my new mission in life!

September 2003—I said I'd be back, so here I am; I'm now nine months from stroke date, and feel obligated to return here. I do feel whole and complete again, so much so that I've begun making personal blunders in my relationships again. I guess it's a good thing to have regained so much confidence that I feel strong enough to voice my true opinions as opposed to meekly sitting back, focusing mostly on my need for certain persons' love and protection. Oh yes, I'm certainly me again, full of self-confidence that disallows anyone from possibly taking advantage of me. I'd really hoped I had learned some life lessons in patience and trust. I hope I have, but I still am human, making mistakes and wishing I could take back words spoken, unthinkingly. Here's a thought: maybe stroke recovery wasn't so bad after all. I sure felt loved and cared for over a long period of time though it was very difficult work, both physically and mentally. So much for feeling whole again! We're just human, all trying to do our best at whatever life throws us!

December 2003 . . . . . Several friends, having read this book draft have mentioned to me that they're anxious to hear about my feeling whole again. I do have moments when I become frustrated at not being able to scoot more quickly across a street when the "walk" flashing light suddenly turns to flashing red-don't-walk. I'm happier when I remember to think about how fortunate I am to even be walking across the street! I am today a much happier and content person than I was before the stroke. I've learned to slow down and take more time to really listen to my precious ten-year-old Trev's stories. I'm so thankful for my new outlook, especially regarding my loved ones. I do feel that because of my stroke, I am truly a better, more thoughtful person. Now this doesn't mean I don't still make lots of mistakes. I allow my old ways of impatience and anger to creep in at the worst times. So I continually feel regret when I've goofed and opened my mouth in anger. At least now I realize that I can be very stubborn and difficult. Before the stroke, I didn't care. I expected people to just "get over it." I'm trying to become a kinder/gentler person these days, and I think that's a pretty great "whole" way of living!

CHAPTER 11

Gripper Socks, Ulus, Dycem, Legal Pads, Clipboards, Grab Bars, and other Tools of the Trade"

It's a Sunday, and I've just finished tidying up my house and my kitchen, so this is a good time to write this chapter! Fortunately, there are available to us, one-handed folks some very helpful tools that assist with getting on with our lives. I've listed the most important ones, to me, above in the title of this chapter. Now, I'll give some simple examples as to what I'm talking about!

Gripper socks: Most of you have either worn these or at the least seen them worn by children. They are warm socks that have a sort of synthetic, flexible, plastic–type cross hatch design (gripper-stuff) on the bottom part (the part you walk on) This gripper material prevents one from slipping on slick floors, such as linoleum floors (found in most hospital rooms), wood floors, and tiled floors. Before I even knew what was happening in the hospital, my feet had been fitted with a fuzzy pair of gripper socks! Luckily, I had a few extra pairs at home that Mike found and brought to me to use during the rest of my hospital stay. You'll get yourself into big trouble with the nurses if you try to move around the hospital room without your gripper socks! I still regularly wear mine at home because they work perfectly for not only keeping my feet warm but also to keep me steady on my linoleum floors.

Ulus: Moving into the kitchen . . . . . a few devices can provide useful help while attempting to get work done in the kitchen. An ulu is a knife, shaped in an arc, (a half circle) attached to a handle. Because using a regular knife is next to impossible and dangerous, using only one hand, the ulu can be used on a cutting board with just your one working hand, giving the one-handed kitchen worker the safe option of cutting food that must be cut with a sharp knife!

Dycem: (pronounced die-some) Keeping to the kitchen . . . this stuff is sticky on two sides—

kind of like the old fly paper strips people
hung from the ceiling to catch flies—and it
comes on a roll, similar to plastic wrap or
aluminum foil. You'll need several pieces
about the size of an 8" by 8" square . . . one
for your kitchen counter and one for your
bathroom counter. The Dycem sheet sticks
to the counter by its sticky underside, yet it
also provides a sticky topside that you will
use throughout the day to provide a stable
and unmovable spot on which you can place
a jar or bottle that needs opened—the bottom of the jar sticks to the dycem, allowing
you to unscrew the lid with one hand! This
stuff is indispensable when it comes to un-
screwing those awful child-resistant caps
used by pharmacies on every medicine bottle
they dispense.

As you can see, in order to retain some semblance of independence, you're going to need
to use these tools in your home!

Legal Pads: Just in case you haven't figured this
out already—I'm a list-maker!

Once I got home, my fingers were just itching to begin my compulsive list-making because there was so much to be taken care of,
especially since I'd been gone from home for
a month! I had already discovered, while in

the hospital, that using a legal pad was my best resource for writing things down. All the pages are attached at the top so that you can write freely with your "good" hand, and when you're done, you can simply and easily tear the finished page from the tablet. Mike even found these great miniature "legal pads" that measure about 6 inches long by 4 inches wide that I can use for my grocery and errands lists! I keep one of these smaller pads by each telephone in my house in case I need to write down a phone message—this is one more un-thought of challenge—writing, while talking on the phone. Yikes! Very difficult to do one-handed. Eventually, however, I've been able to accomplish this task with a lot of practice. At first when I got home, I used my teenage daughter's hands-free phone headset (She graciously removed it from its seemingly permanently attached spot on her ears!). I suggest that you ask someone in your family to go shopping for a new hands-free headset telephone for you to use when you get home!

Clipboards: Another handy device for writing and keeping pieces of paper in place.

I discovered early on that we unconsciously use both hands while writing—one hand is

writing while the other holds the paper in
place so it doesn't move as the writing hand
moves across the paper! I'd truly never
thought about this until after the stroke when
I realized how difficult it was to even perform what used to be the simple task of writing checks to pay my bills. Because this is so
difficult and frustrating, as I suggested earlier in the book, it's a really good idea to ap-
point a trusted friend to become your
personal secretary! Taylor, my sixteen-year-
old daughter, and I used this opportunity as
a "teachable moment"—I taught her how to
write checks and keep a running total of
funds available in the register—all I had to
do was sign the checks. Several months after I returned home, we set up Taylor's own
checking account for her to use to pay for
her own car expenses.

Grab Bars: While in the hospital, you'll learn all
about the necessity of grab bars in the bathroom. One of the first moves you make towards recovery is to get up out of bed and
move to the wheelchair in order to have a
nurse wheel you into the bathroom. The
medical terminology for this "move" is called
a "transfer." You are taught to first get yourself upright on your bed from a lying down

position—it's absolutely amazing how suddenly this seemingly simple movement has now become a major exercise in coordination! Then you move to a standing position—another feat of power! Then you are ready for the transfer. The nurses and therapists teach you to use your strong leg to pivot around so your backside is in position to sit "carefully" into the wheelchair—No free-falling allowed! You'll then be wheeled to the toilet where you're expected to perform yet one more superwoman feat—stand up, pivot, and sit on the toilet without losing your balance and falling! This is where the grab bars come in. You quickly learn to reach and hold on to the bar to steady your suddenly unbalanced body and use the strength in your good arm to help yourself be able to sit on the toilet.

Also grab bars become completely necessary in the shower and bathtub, Your OT will teach you to use the grab bars while in the shower at the hospital. Before I left for home, my OT and I practiced using the grab bars to pull myself up and out of the sitting position while in a bathtub, so that once I returned home, I could again enjoy a warm bath!

Again, who else, but my wonderful Mike "in his spare time" had gone and purchased and installed grab bars for my bathtub/shower at home!

Pumper Bottles: The stroke patient is probably going to have to perform all tasks with just the use of one hand, so being able to easily dispense—all by herself—regularly used liquids, such as lotion, shampoo, and conditioner, and body wash is a very important accomplishment. One of my wonderful nurses, Ramanda, suggested this idea after she had helped me during several shower sessions—it became very apparent to her that I could be much more self-sufficient if I could dispense, by myself, my shower toiletries!

Purchasing empty pumper bottles and then filling each one with the stroke patient's favorite shower choices would be the perfect "hospital gift!" While Mike and I were out-on-pass on one of our Christmas shopping trips, we found and purchased a "pumper-dispenser that attaches to the wall inside my shower at home. I continue to happily use the dispenser today, < 4 ° months from stroke> and it looks so pretty filled with purple/lavender shampoo, conditioner, and body wash!

Elastic/coiled shoe strings: My therapists at the hospital introduced me to these special little wonders. Of course, the stroke patient can no longer tie her shoes because, as I so often put it "that's a two-hand job! These elastic laces come in mainly black or white; however, I do remember finding some wild multi-colored ones for Taylor's shoes when she was a toddler, and I wanted her to be able to put on her own shoes without the worry of lacing them up. Your tennis shoes will be the best shoes to wear while in therapy, so of course, you'll need a pair of elastic laces in order to get yourself dressed, all on your own, each day.

Thank God that all these helpful tools are available to encourage independence for the stroke recovering person!

CHAPTER 12

My Own Stroke Story "Don't it always seem to go that you don't know what you got till it's gone?"

Tami, we think you've had a stroke, one of the paramedics said to me during the quick ride in the ambulance on the way to the emergency room. And that was my first realization that I was indeed in trouble. It was a Wednesday early morning, and I had arrived at Workout West at 4:45 A.M. as I had done every Monday, Wednesday, and Friday mornings over the past seven years. My routine was to complete my quick 15 minute "weight-lifting workout" prior to joining my 45 to 60 (depending on the day) workout buddies for the 5:00 A.M. one-hour Bootcamp class, led by our fearless 95 pounds of pure muscle and heart leader, Kim—We all used to call her "killer Kim," but since my stroke, that title isn't so funny any longer to any of us! Class began, and Kim took us through the initial full group warm-up. Then she instructed us to breakout into our smaller groups of fours in order to begin the circuit stations. My buddy, Roda, and I had invited a new person to join our group, and we three had begun our first pushups station. Roda has always kept me thoroughly entertained during class with her funny stories and humor, and that day was no different. I was listening to Roda's story as I began my pushups against the raised instructor's platform. Then, as part of the station exercise, it was time to jump up on the platform to do the knee raise. Roda and I jumped up at the same time, did our knee raises; then we jumped backwards down to the floor to repeat our pushups. When we both put our arms forward to catch the platform, my right arm slipped so that I fell slightly to the right, off balanced.

Because we have all experienced little slips and trips during the routinely fast-paced station rotations, Roda giggled, thinking that I had simply slipped and somehow missed connecting with the platform.

She looked over at me, laughing and asked, "Are you okay?" Since I thought I was, I said, "I'm okay, but my fingers are all numb." Actually, when I spoke, I knew that something besides numb fingers was happening, and I felt a bit light-headed. When I heard myself answer Roda, my voice sounded very slow and slurred, and it was difficult for me to speak. I decided I would just walk it off and take some deep breaths, so I walked over to the water fountain to get a drink. Now, I do not remember exactly all the following details, but here is what I do remember; again thinking that my fingers felt strange and numb, I began to walk back to Roda in order to continue with the next station, but I didn't make it. Kim stopped me, inquiring, "Tami, are you all right?" Again, my speech sounded slurred, "I think I'm okay; my fingers are numb, though." Kim sounded very concerned, "Well, you're kind of hugging the wall there, so I think we better get you down to rest on the floor!" She immediately enlisted helpers to keep me down on the floor to rest, and I heard her say in a very worried tone, "Dave, we have a situation here!" Lynda had gently suggested that I lean back into her to relax, which I did because by that time, I was scared I was going to faint. Kim said, "Now Tami, you just relax; we've got an ambulance on the way." I thought to myself, "I've just got a flu bug, you guys; quit making such a big deal of this!" I said, "I don't want an ambulance!"

Dr. Kelly Tucker, another workout buddy, came over and said, "Tami, just relax; we've got help coming, and we're going to get you to the hospital." Next thing I knew, the paramedics were introducing themselves to me, saying that they needed to get an IV into my arm. I thought, "Oh great, here we go, an expensive ambulance ride, and I'm just fine."

Thank God I was among caring and quick-thinking friends. Roda began asking me for Mike's phone number, and I was able to give her some information—enough that she phoned Mike, telling him that she'd meet him in the emergency room. The paramedics lifted me onto the gurney and carried me out the doors to the awaiting ambulance! I remember thinking, "Gosh, I need to stay awake here.

I've never had an ambulance ride before!"

The next thing I remember is being carried into the emergency room (Chapter 2).

CHAPTER 13

A Six Month
Hump-date!

There's more to write! The therapists and doctors talk about the difficulties of reaching plateaus during the progress time from the stroke, but here I am six months from my stroke, and I honestly don't feel as if I've yet to reach a point when my progress has come to a standstill. Honestly, I think my positive outlook has helped me continue to strive forward on a daily basis and to continually add new exercises to my at-home therapy follow-through. However, I must admit to feeling a bit burned out this morning, not wanting to change into my swimsuit and drive to the pool! I decided I needed a little pep talk, so I thought to myself, "Hey, if I weren't headed to the pool, I'd be heading to work about now. I just need to remember that this therapy is actually my job right now, so get to work!"

It worked! I went to the pool and swam my laps for 60 minutes, and I'm so glad I did because that warm water always nicely loosens up my muscles and joints!

Six months is a long time, especially when you're doing some of the hardest work you'll ever do in your life. The toughest part at this point is keeping a positive outlook for the future, but as I've said earlier, it sure helps to keep in mind all the good things that have happened over the last six months and to remind myself about how far I've come since being in a hospital bed, not knowing whether I'd even be able to walk again.

May 14th I'm back with more great news! The sun has been shining, warming the cool Colorado spring weather for three days straight! This miracle along with my daily outings has been just the ticket to boost my spirits.

I'm moving back into advice mode now! STAY ACTIVE . . . Meet with co-workers by visiting your workplace and checking back in . . . . meet good friends for "chatty" lunches . . . . . get out of the house and do errands by yourself . . . (grocery store, vehicle maintenance, etc.) make therapy and exercise your number-one top priority five days each week . . . relax on the weekends with your special someone! This is exactly what I have done since returning home from the hospital, and I truly think that my activities combined with the now sunny, warm weather can be credited with my "sunny outlook" for the next few months! I am realizing how very close I am now coming to the completion of my journey to 100% recovery. Of course, I have a summer ahead filled with tons of therapy and exercise, but even this morning when I walked out of the therapy pool, a woman whom I have yet to meet, commented on my improvement! Therapy and exercise work toward stroke recovery when a person persistently sticks with it as I have!

Continue doing the menial jobs at home that were your responsibility before the stroke! Today, I cleaned out and organized the refrigerator, unplugged Trev's toilet with the hand-dandy plunger, and picked up the assorted marbles that my two-year-old nephew had scattered in Trev's room while Peggy and I visited!

I can't emphasize enough how capable I feel when these simple, accomplished tasks are completed. As I've suggested before, we must pat ourselves on the backs for any and all accomplishments "after stroke." My children still see me as their ever-capable mom—not an invalid.

June 16—I'm baaaak! I must admit I've been so busy with Trev since school let out that I haven't been able to get back here in several weeks; however, I have excellent progress to report! I am now at 6 ° months from stroke, and, honestly, the disabilities on my left side, today, are simply, only a minor inconvenience—I no longer feel like a stroke victim! My life has truly returned to some normalcy. I'm able to walk with a very close to normal gait; I can lift my left arm above my head; I have regained strength and stamina so that I can make it through a full day of activities without feeling absolutely exhausted! I continue therapy several times each week (I pay for my therapy out of my own funds since my HMO insurance won't pay for therapy any longer) to work on regaining control over my wrist and fingers; I'm confident that control is coming soon. I still have seven weeks of summer to work at this before my return to work, and I've learned over these last months that what does work is persistence and hard work! So that's exactly what I'm going to do!

CHAPTER 14

8,9,10,11,12 Months Out

I feel obligated to be extremely honest. Things have not gone exactly according to my plans. Although not one doctor nor therapist ever told me that I would be recovered from the stroke by the summer, I had decided that was when I was going to be recovered. I'll warn you that the doctors and therapists very carefully will not estimate about recovery dates, and as I've discovered, they have good reasons for such non-committal stands. Every stroke is completely different, and there is no possible way to estimate how or when someone's brain and body finally recover. Whew, this requires extreme patience.

Summer is nearly over; My kids go back to school this week, and I am certainly not at 100% recovery . . . yet! However, what I am . . . is back to work and functioning in the real world, though my physical recovery is seemingly moving at a snail's pace or so it seems to me. My natural walking gait has not returned . . . yet, nor do I have complete control of my left arm, hand, and fingers . . . yet.

Nevertheless, I have experienced substantial progress: I've regained strength and stamina; I returned to my job part-time in July (8 months after stroke!) and now in August, I work all day long without requiring a nap, and I love being at work; I have completely recovered from the rotator cuff injury as I can now lift and/or push 25 pounds of weight at the gym without pain! Also, it no longer takes me 90 minutes to shower and dress. In many ways, I'm back to my life as it was pre-stroke. I've been able to take each of my children for their day-long, back-to-school clothes shopping excursions. I get up very early, three mornings each week to go workout and can tie the laces in my tennis shoes (very slowly), and I join boot-camp for the final 15 minute abdominal workout and finishing stretch, after I have completed my one-hour individual workout that includes 30 minutes of cardiovascular work on the stair-master and 30 minutes of weight/strength training!

The point I'm trying to make is that though I'm not 100% recovered by my own timeline, I'm daily progressing. It's a painstakingly slow battle done persistently on a daily basis. I'm still convinced I'll see 100% recovery some day; I just am not sure when, but I am sure that the only way to get there is to "work it" every single day, never giving in or letting go of the goal!

After all, I don't even need or use the dycem any longer in order to open bottles or jars; I can now hold bottles/jars, etc. in my left hand and open them with my right hand; granted, it's not like it used to be; each action that involves both hands is difficult and slow, but I get it done! I'm sure with time and practice, the ease will return, just like my stamina and strength have returned.

Eight months out, I believe more than ever the key to recovery is *HOPE* and never giving up, but continuing to work at recovery constantly. I continue to see either Kryste or Chris once each week for a therapy session which I've chosen to pay for myself from my savings since my HMO no longer will pay for stroke recovery. What better way to use my savings account than for my own recovery?

NINE-MONTH REPORT

Again, I must be terribly honest in that what I must report is somewhat negative; however, I think that the fact that this is happening is proof that my life is in fact my own again! My close friends, family, and I have noticed that my patience and tolerance for others has definitely shortened. When I saw myself as a recovering stroke victim, I lived my days in a manner of thankfulness for everything and everyone, and that was a very good way to live/recover . . . positive and loving! Now, however, I don't feel so generous; I'm back to standing up for myself and losing my patience when *I perceive* stupidity, stubbornness, or ignorance. In other words, I once again am back to my old ways of expecting much more out of others than just a smile and words of encouragement. I become intolerant and angry these days when someone says or does something that pushes my buttons. Now, I'm not completely out-of-control; I am capable of zipping the lips and not voicing outright exactly what I'm thinking.

People, this ability or confidence to speak out is a sure sign of life-back to-normal for me! I've always been the type of person to say exactly what I think needs to be said, and yes, I've wished many times to take back those words. This is a personality trait I lost with the natural loss of confidence that the stroke imposes, but I think this return is a sure sign of life-back-to-normal for me, however, positive or negative it might prove in the long haul. Whew, this is a tough turn in the road, but progress, nonetheless.

On a more positive note, the physical progress continues on a daily basis, though, for me it still feels like a snail's pace. A friend at boot-camp made a wonderful observation. Nelle said, "Tami, it's just like we all react to seeing children as they grow; if we haven't seen children for nine months or a year, we are amazed at their growth and how much they've changed, yet their own family members, living with them daily shrug their shoulders and ask, 'What changes? They're just naturally growing up!'" It can be so encouraging when others comment about your progress, though it may seem so minimal to yourself.

The really big transition during this ninth month has been my return to full-time work.

THE TENTH MONTH

I'm still typing one-handed, but I've become pretty darned good at it! As I write this morning, it is 5:24 A.M., and I cannot sleep. My mind generally wakes up and kicks in these days about 4:00 A.M., another sure sign of recovery . . . . What a pain. I've talked to a few other people who have had strokes, and they also seem to have the lack-of-sleep problem; in fact a good restful sleep is hard to come by. I'm sure there are hundreds of medical reasons that hundreds of doctors could each expound their own individual theories. But I really don't care about the reasons; I just know it's difficult these days to wake up feeling really rested. However, I'm not complaining! I must admit that before the stroke, I generally would wake up early, before sunrise, and I liked it that way because I could get a lot more done during the day, so this return to my old ways is a good thing for me. I was worried at one point in the hospital when my natural inner-alarm didn't wake me up until breakfast-time! Oh well—another return back to my life-before-stroke is a good indication that life as I want to live it will be mine again!

I've been fairly introspective over the last few weeks, and one outstanding thought is that I'm so grateful that I began this book five months ago because if I were to try to sit down today and try to write those first twelve chapters, I'd have a very difficult time—in fact, I couldn't remember all the important details I've been able to share so far.

I encouraged earlier in the book, to engage yourself in your passion; this book (my passion) is growing along with my recovery, and it will, therefore, always represent a very dear piece of my life. What a wonderful symbol for me to have for years to come from this incredible stroke experience!

It's 5:00 A.M. again, and I've been feeling the "need" to get back here to report! Again, I'm so thankful for this passion of mine to return to often;

I can't state passionately enough how very important to healthy recovery it is to incorporate your own
personal passion into your daily life! If not for this
book in which to lose myself at times, I might become depressed and unhappy because this stroke
recovery takes a l aaaaa aawwng t i m e. But recovery does happen if you stick with it and keep the
spirits up!

I'm now nearing my 11th month, and when I
walked down the stairs this morning, from my bed-
room to get here to my little desk-haven, I realized
that my left leg actually just feels like I remember
my body used to feel after I'd pushed too hard or
over-exerted at bootcamp or weight-lifting workout—that same muscle tightness or soreness. Heck,
I used to do that on a weekly basis, so I can certainly deal with living with a sore left side. BECAUSE
life is a wonderful gift, and I'm so glad I'm here to
live it—I'm not satisfied to sit back and watch everyone else living the show—I intend to fully take
part, and you should too! Don't give up now—there's
so much life to live!

I must emphasize how terribly important it is to
get back to work, being engaged in your career, being productive! Mike and I have stayed in touch with
a fellow stroke patient, Bob and his wife, Debbie,
and we've been thrilled recently to see them out
having Sunday morning breakfast. It's taken Bob a

little longer than me to recover, physically, but only because Bob is the typical successful businessman. He is in his fifties, and probably wasn't in his top physical condition when the stroke struck. Bob has in the last few months returned to serving on some very influential Advisory Boards in our little city. People still seek out his keen mind, and innate sense for knowing how/when/where/ and whom to get-things done. We've all seen a marked improvement in Bob's physical ability since returning to "work." Bob now only requires a walking stick, and refuses to use the wheelchair! In fact he was very proud to tell me that at a recent function, he refused the offer to bring the microphone to his seat, but rather he stood up from the head table, climbed several steps to the podium, and gave his speech! What a mind he has, and he is productively sharing his gifts with our community. He's not giving up! even though it's now been ten long months, and complete physical recovery is on its way.

I've been so blessed as a result of this stroke, especially by the new people I've met and can now count as close, dear friends. Life has so much to offer; I shudder to think of the alternative in giving up because it's just too hard of work. The hard work allows the return to an even better life than before. I won't go so far to say I'm glad I had the stroke, but Wow, I'm certainly grateful for the lessons I've learned. As I enter my 11ᵗʰ month of stroke recovery, my future days seem awfully bright, and I can't wait to see the new adventures just waiting out there to happen!

TWELVE MONTHS . . . A WHOLE AMAZING YEAR

It's Thanksgiving, November 27, 2003—quite an emotion-packed day for me. I can't stress enough the joy I feel today. I am so happy with my life, and I'm so glad this year is behind me and that I now move on with one year of stroke recovery solidly under my belt! I thank God daily for the return of my life and the fact that He has chosen to allow me to actively participate in my children's lives. Mike and I are now engaged and planning our marriage and future life together—I just can't imagine how life could be any better.

Now, readers, I am not yet at 100% recovery, and it truly doesn't matter because I now understand that those days will come down the road. I have learned a patience level that I didn't think was possible. Our brains are incredibly intricate; therefore, recovery to a brain injury, such as a CVA comes only after an amazing number of repetitions that can only happen over long periods of time. Already, during these last several months(9, 10, 11, & 12) I have watched with amazement as the return of simple movements come back to me, but only after I've exerted the effort to perform that movement, probably at least 400 times (that means every day since stroke, folks). I'm confident now in saying that the key to recovery must be never—ever giving up, trying to perform that difficult movement every single day. Now, there's no surprising miracles happening here. Every day it just gets a tiny bit easier, until one day you perform the movement, and it doesn't completely wipe you out as it did the first, second, third . . . . etc. times that you tried to perform the task!

Here's a great example! Opening a door with your hand on your stroke side. I clearly remember those first times here at home when I attempted to open the door that leads to/from my garage, usually because I had my right hand/arm full of stuff I was carrying, either trying to get out to the car or trying to get inside from the garage with my right arm full of groceries! I reached out with my left hand and nearly turned my body upside down with the effort to simply turn the doorknob and open the door with my left hand, but I kept trying every day, even though there were many times I just gave up, setting down the load from my right arm in order to open the door with my right hand. Guess what happened just one hour ago!? I carried/juggled from my car a sack of yummy Thanksgiving leftovers and a crockpot with leftover mashed potatoes that I took to our family Thanksgiving feast. While holding onto all that stuff, I opened the door with my left hand, stuck out my left foot to hold the darned, self-closing, hinged door into the house, and I made it in without dropping or breaking anything! These accomplishments are worthy of great hurrahs!—I continue to give myself daily pats on the back for simple tasks in which I've succeeded, taking special delight in my amazing body as it re-learns. It's so much more fun to be happy about simple tasks accomplished rather than sitting down in a crying self-pity heap!

I'm so much happier when I'm trying rather than choosing not to try. I have to be honest that tying my shoes is one task that I've not really given my best effort to on a daily basis; unfortunately, I decided that I just wasn't going to expend the effort at 4:00 A.M. on my workout mornings to tie my tennis shoes—I cheated by asking Mike to tie them tightly for me one morning, and then I proceeded to stuff the bows down under the tightened laces so that, like many children also do, I take off and put back on my shoes without ever unlacing them. Now, I'm regretting that choice because if I'd pushed myself to tie those darned laces three mornings each week, I know that by now because of that repetition, I'd be tying my laces with little effort. I'm making a new year's resolution right now to start tying those laces on workout mornings, and I'm sure that by this time next year, I'll be tying my shoes again as if I never had a stroke!

I realize now that stroke recovery is probably a rest-of-my-life journey—oh well—I am now daily thankful and so much more observant of all I do have to be thankful for, and I prefer living life with a thankful attitude as opposed to the hurry-up-everybody attitude I lived before stroke.

Thank you, God, for allowing my family and me this incredible journey . . . . .

Appendix A

While sorting through some drawers in my office, I came across my Thank you letter that I sent out to everyone who had given me gifts during and after my hospital stay, and I think it was such a great way to thank everyone that I'll share it here. I simply typed it on the computer, printed them on pretty paper, then Mike and Trev helped me fold, stuff, seal, and stamp envelopes! Many people responded so pleased with my simple little thank you gesture. I suggest trying this if you have 100's of thank-you's to send as I did!*******************************

February 2003

I have chosen to express my gratitude to each of you through this "update" note as it is so very important to me that you know how much I have appreciated your prayers and thoughts over the last months. The beautiful cards, flowers, plants, meals, and special gifts have brightened my days! I was released from the hospital on December 23, just in time to spend Christmas with my kids and family. Since that point, we have settled somewhat into being back home.

I know that many of you have wondered how I spend my days at home, after having been so busy so much of my life. Actually, I'm learning to slow down and relax a bit, and I'm enjoying the quiet time that I can catch up on my reading.

Also, my kids continue to keep me on my toes. Dustin checks in with me regularly to give me updates on his classes at CSU.

Taylor and Trevor are with me every day after school, and stay with me three nights each week; they are with Oscar the other three nights, and we alternate weekends. This schedule has continued to work wonderfully for all of us over the last three years. I see the kids every day, and they are with their Dad regularly also. Trev has basketball games every Saturday and indoor soccer on Sundays. Taylor turned 16 on December 19, and her Aunt Beth was so special in making sure Tay got her driver's license that very day. In November, Tay bought my sister Peggy's used Honda with her own hard-earned lawn mowing money, and fortunately, she and I purchased plates and insurance right away, so she has been my best little helper, making grocery store runs, picking up Trev after school, and just getting us around town for errands. My doctors have just recently released me to drive, so I now look forward to getting around independently. Meanwhile, I've been going to therapy two to three times each week; Mike usually takes me, and he continues to be my main support. What an amazing guy he is. God knew exactly what he was doing when he brought Mike into my life. Throughout these last months, Mike has been right by my side, loving and caring for me, so that I've not felt scared or hopeless. Thank God for Mike!

I am healing with therapy and hard work. I now realize how fortunate I've been with a strong, healthy body all my life. Re-learning such simple things like walking, bending my elbow, wrist, and fingers has become the focus of my days.

Besides these amazing feats, patience and the "art" of taking things slowly are also sinking into my brain. I am learning a much more grateful way of living life, not taking anyone or anything for granted; again, I want to be sure you know how very much I appreciate your kindness to me during this time. I am daily getting back more energy and stamina.

When I have visited with friends, most have asked about my financial situation. Again, I must credit God's hand in the bigger picture of my life. My job at UNC provided me with excellent benefits, from medical insurance that has covered the majority of those expenses and sick leave that has provided me with a monthly paycheck. I am not struggling in any way, just happy to be alive and getting better. It's looking as though I will not be ready to return to work until fall and the next school year . . . This rehab is a long, tedious process; but I'm thankful for all those pushups and sit-ups I accomplished at early morning "bootcamp" exercise all those years! That residual muscle tone helps while my poor brain works to remember how to send messages to those muscles. What an amazing challenge I've had placed in front of me . . . I'm happy and getting better every day!

To order additional copies of

UNFORTUNATE
STROKE
LUCK

Have your credit card ready and call:

1-877-421-READ (7323)

or please visit our web site at
www.pleasantword.com

Also available at:
www.amazon.com
and
www.barnesandnoble.com

Printed in the United States
203567BV00001B/76-78/A